Coconut Palm Kind of Woman

poems by

Nimi Finnigan

Finishing Line Press
Georgetown, Kentucky

Coconut Palm Kind of Woman

*For Ayiti Cherie,
Always. Forever.*

Copyright © 2016 by Nimi Finnigan
ISBN 978-1-944899-39-4 First Edition
All rights reserved under International and Pan-American Copyright Conventions. No part of this book may be reproduced in any manner whatsoever without written permission from the publisher, except in the case of brief quotations embodied in critical articles and reviews.

ACKNOWLEDGMENTS

Many thanks to the periodicals where these poems initially appeared, sometimes in slightly different versions:
"Moving to Lubbock Texas," and "A Skill for Us Black Folk" in *The Meadowland Review*
"A Cotton Field in Crosbyton Texas," "Pittsburgh Dust," and "Funeral Smoke: the Lower Ninth Ward" in the *Journal of Caribbean Literature*.

Thank you to everyone at Finishing Line Press for making a dream come true.

Special thanks to my mentors, teachers, and fellow writers: Anna Catone, Sandy Sterner, Sheryl St.Germain, Heather McNaugher, all of you kept me in love with poetry; and Jackie Kolosov, Henrietta Goodman, your on-going support for this collection filled me with inspiration and insight for which I am eternally grateful.

Most of all, thank you to my extraordinary family—Mousson Pierre, Sean Finnigan, Leah Reed, Eri Seta, Roderick Vann, and my daughters. Love doesn't even begin to cover it.

Editor: Christen Kincaid
Cover Art: Sean Finnigan
Author Photo: Sean Finnigan
Cover Design: Elizabeth Maines

Printed in the USA on acid-free paper.
Order online: www.finishinglinepress.com
        also available on amazon.com

Author inquiries and mail orders:
Finishing Line Press
P. O. Box 1626
Georgetown, Kentucky 40324
U. S. A.

Table of Contents

Part I
Moving to Lubbock, Texas 1
My Grandmother Explained How I Was This "Sugared Woman" 3
The Shape of Emptiness 4
Mama's Warning 6
13 Months in Lubbock, Texas and Shopping for Toilet Paper, Plaintains, Clorox Wipes and Castor Oil 7
A Skill for Us Black Folk 8
Blanc—"Foreigner" 9
Pittsburgh Dust 10

Part II
Miscarriage 12
Behind Molotov Cocktails 14
On Hearing Eric Clapton's Guitar in a Small Village in the South of Haiti 15
"My Skin Folk Ain't My Kin Folk" 17
Like Sunken Coal 19
Funeral Smoke: The Lower Ninth Ward, Louisiana 20
"Holds Me like a Heaven" 21
A Cotton Field in Crosbyton Texas 23

Part III
Song for Making the Birds Come 26
Mojito Love, After Hurricane Katrina 27
Move on moonlight, this is just another failed love poem ... 28
In the Backyard 29
A Couple of Halves 30
Twilight. Layette, Louisiana 31
For Erzuli, Goddess of Love 32
Our Road of Song 33
Une Nuit sur une Plage Haitienne 34

Part I

Moving to Lubbock, Texas

I say to myself: do not do this.

You are a coconut palm kind of woman.
The foremilk of the hard-shelled seed,

so pale, so necessary,
the meat lining is never nourishment enough.

You know about coconuts, the kind frog-men steal,
slithering up and down brown heights,

thighs wrapped tight,
muscles more sculpted mounds than flesh.

You have been taught that frog-men pick the best coconuts.
It's almost intimate, this knowing.

Now picture coconuts growing fat beside cotton bolls,
each one a miniature soul, cloud-like and dry-heaving

West Texas dust back into the air, your lungs.
Reminisce history into this present drought,

the black-grape skins raisining in the sun
for a hundred pounds of cloud-blossoms,

and your grandmother enters, living through layers of pain
because there are pieces of cotton in the aspirin bottles;

and the leaves and mountains of the island enter,
their boiling shades of green.

They hear the man with the machete,
the slow approach of the homemade blade

And the island light? It stays harsh
so contours are embossed loud. Light living on the edge.

So you tell yourself moving down here is not the thing to do
because you are cultivated coconut palm-like, thick, brown and fibrous,

and flowering continuously with the blood red bougainvillea,
always transitioning from flower to fire; and married to the violence

of the island in such a tender fashion,
what you know of survival might not take root anywhere else.

My Grandmother Explained How I Was This "Sugared Woman"

My grandmother sang about the molasses
between my thighs, told me my empty womb
wept because of the moon, because of the pale
grey churning my insides with salt.

The moon tide between my thighs flavored
all things red, she said, with a scent of rice
ripened over the heat of garlic and wild parsley.

The flesh sweetness—she breathed in my ear—of the moon
scalded the small of my back
so that these brown sugar aches
found their way out of me as fresh honey, my own.

This city veils the moon in a northern silk
of confectioner's sugar and between my thighs,
the molasses still throbs, Grandmother,

but with the scent of snow and soot,
cramps over smoke and rockwater.

The Shape of Emptiness

You would think it would be hard
to poetry your way into West Texas

but these here plains,
goldenrod-dyed and rainless,

are begging for words.
The tornado dust storms pick up

language and whittle it down, whittle it
to one sound, what you fear most,

the shape of your own emptiness
like the horizon, never quite coming

but so clearly crimson.
Texas holds Haiti.

Not in the sky—the cerulean
stain is too blue, too immaculate.

The island is in the wind.
Listen.

Doesn't it remind you of your body?
Parts of you—follicles, epidermis—

heavy with coconut and castor oil, the slick films
of youth that greased your skin in 1982.

The curves of the island moan through
the canyons, and in one slow bellow,

the desert, the hiss of the ocean, the Walmarts
they all hush up into something,

an unfurled solitude,
the size of a pinprick.

Mama's Warning

Don't go strollin' over
the dark man's cabbage field, little girl.

He likes red cabbage.

His face, the back of his palms
are molasses and stick to shoes, skirt, skin.

Little girl,
the dark man's keys rattlesnake his front pocket.

He plants red cabbage
for mid-summer,
these almost purple leaves
he can grow between your thighs.

13 Months in Lubbock, Texas, and Shopping for Toilet Paper, Plaintains, Clorox Wipes, and Castor Oil

Bovine loneliness and bovine shit
bleed through the navigable sorrow
of Wal-Mart's sliding doors.
Much like the snail I crushed
this morning, loneliness exists here.
It goes beyond the vibrato
of eardrums, beyond sound.
It's a silence with a beat.
Hold yourself, cup your breast.
Both of them. Hear it through hands, palms,
burrowing through veins where the blood is slow,
where it teaches the body the art of lingering.
This city's liquid stench knows how to drown,
pushes through the surface of you,
the snail's gelatinous body, the crack
of her mollusk shell, the only sound.

A Skill for Us Black Folk

You taught me to chew it, Grandma.
That word: cotton. Make my taste buds recognize it.

A necessary skill for us black folk.

A field came upon me the other day, in the lost planes
of Lubbock, Texas, so flat, so quiet, I came face-to-face
with the cotton after-taste of our entire people.
All those things you said were inescapable.

And in the air, a bird. Perhaps an eagle.
Browner than my skin, wings stretched over the field, skillful.
The cotton bolls reached for her, Grandma,
and caught only a weightless shade, drifting.

Blanc—"Foreigner"
~ *On leaving Haiti for the first time*

I remember American Airlines flight 803
and Lt. Jarvis on his way from almost bombing
grandfather's backyard. He whispered

creole is a dialect not a language
across my chest, clicked
my seat belt into place.

The cabbies called me Sista
in Flatbush, Sista in East Liberty.
I offered plantain and bread fruit

and they remembered the four H's
HIV, Heroin, Homosexual, Haitian.
My tongue gnarled *cherry vanilla*

Dr. Pepper into syllabled morsels,
staccato slow, when Bob, Pittsburgh Public
Safety officer, sang of the occupation,

how quickly a body
of people surrendered,
his best memory of 1968.

Before I left, my father said
we reclaimed the Land of Moutains,
christened it Ayiti.

A la bel Ayiti Cheri bel!

Waiting for the 71 C in-bound,
at the corner of Fifth and Tennyson,
I remember.

Pittsburgh Dust

East Liberty's December sky
drapes razor sharp ice patterns
over her eyelids

and silver burns a latticework
of snow over the charcoal
contours of her face.

She aches Haitian for the aroma
of burnt coffee. Arabica smoke, undistilled.
Offers her throat to the city's sorrowful wind.

But the snowflakes still marble
sidewalks of sleet across
her swollen lips.

She traps the taste of cold
and Downtown grime beneath
her tongue, and swallows.

Part II

Miscarriage

My body was coal.
Made of the dark
stuff of the island
chocolate soot, bitter
but native sweetened,
and thick.

But I am quickening.

The body inside my body
has slowed, the heartbeat
marking time, stiffening
seconds into hours into
an unfamiliar monster.

Sluggish quiverings
quiet the air.

Flecks of ash and dust
sink to the un-green
ground, magnify and ribbon
into spirits, into women
from the old tales, my grandmother.

Ghostly graces spill
from their pipe-smoke
lengths, their mouths.

Listen, the women say.

Listen to the motionless
murmur of your womb.
Mother the tiny dying
melody until it recedes
into memory and sea-mist.

But listening to my child
die is breathing in snow.
A swarm of sour echoes
crowds my living room.

I sink toward the beige carpet
fibers. Fissures unlacing my skin.
I ripen with the silence,

and a downpour of hexes
coil inside me, shadows
breaking loose.

I want to rage in the abyss,
rave my soul chaffing
against God, the fates,
their decision to unglobe
my belly, petrify my daughter's
name in the back of my throat
make her a small stone
I never swallow.

Behind Molotov Cocktails

*On hearing about the young Haitian boys who are captured and
brainwashed into committing escalating acts of violence*

They pour the liquid into glass containers,
beer bottles and rhum bottles, Barbancourts
that shatter purple, green and blue,
before wall and flame and someone's handkerchief embrace,

and combust so that the house you built with your wife
the neighbors, the colors you used
red, blue to gloss over the stubbled edges of raw cement,
the scent of paint

always better than the smell of ground earth,
all the memories blanketed across the mud-brown tiles,
everything, in one breath, blooms into this single flower,

this cluster of heat and light and kerosene, petals writhing.
Behind this aftermath of your soul
and your home exploding

is this miniature black-brown clan,
a forest of reed-wild children,
boys with coconut-hard-bellies.

Their hunger growing limbs beneath their dust-mud skin.

On Hearing Eric Clapton's Guitar in a Small Village in the South of Haiti
~ *For the young boys behind the rifles*

I

Joseph learnt from a "natif natal,"
a night-skinned man from fish-gutting sand folk,
a shanti citizen, a man
who knows how a tin roof
can incubate sunlight, and then scald
and cleave the epidermis from muscle,
so that what you sweat is not salt
but skin on the mud-floor
of a one-roomed house.

The night-skinned man mines the raw
shapelessness of an 8 year-old's wrath, polishes it
militia-like because the night-skinned man knows
policemen are fathers, soldiers are fathers,
even the *blancs* of the navy seal, the American night ghosts,
they too will all pause before pulling the trigger on a child.

The night-skinned man inducts boys
into the fire-sweetness of the Molotov cocktail
and the sawed down rifle, only the gifted like Joseph
graduate to the semi-automatic's staccato.

II

When Joseph heard that *blanc*, that one time
on the palm-sized television in the village store,
Joseph's body tremored past the sound
of the wounded strings, his thieving potbelly paused,
tremored, and then synchronized with the stringed moan
of the brown-haired white man's guitar.

That one time Joseph tucked himself under the mango trees,
orchard shades no one can find but a little boy,
Joseph stuck a thick reed into the mouth
of an empty kerosene can, cradled his makeshift guitar
and accompanied Eric Clapton, eyes closed
to the noon butter light.

On his face, a smile so soft, the orchard bloomed.

"My Skin Folk Ain't My Kin Folk"
~ Zora Neale Hurston

No siren song here, there is
only a whisper, broken
and barely carried on the wind.
Africa does not rumble in our ear,
the sound of those shores drowned
out, long ago. Their motion stilled
when the marooned slave and Indian
Taino mouthed "Ayiti." In unison.

The mother land hushed.

You know the echo I am talking about.
The one that laces the ear, the one
that magnetizes the insides of so many
of my skin folk.

But here, veins and arteries rhythm
to Haiti's Macaya mountains,
the island's bumps and bruises.
It's the nation's jazz snaking the blood, red,
the konpa beat tattooing itself
across our limbs, birthing islanders.

Kin folk with mango skins between their teeth,
the peel purple and proud, swaying like a flag
from their open mouths, and the words of Joj Kastra
waiting loud on their tongue:

*An n'al gade sans koule
cheri,
se soley ki pral couche*

*Let's go see blood flow
darling,
the sun is setting.*

Like Sunken Coal

To lose words, not one by one but decibel by decibel
until conversations are clothed in petal-soft
shouts, until all that is left is a static

so silken the space between our mouths
could not trouble breeze or candle-flame.
Our last syllables not subtle, not fever-pitched wild

but wet with a doomed breath,
a careless hollow of husks.

Funeral Smoke: The Lower Ninth Ward, Louisiana
　~ *After Katrina*

There are days when silence tastes like silver ashes.
Freshly blown and hovering, almost stagnant but in the air.
Flakes of tobacco wrap around the heat, swallow it.

And then there is the moment, the minute when the flakes
should move, just before they move to kiss the ground
or dissipate into some leaf, but don't...

That minute, that hour, in black and white, perhaps even grey,
when the smoke slides off a cracked
lower lip, and behind the silence exposes a cry.

"Holds Me like a Heaven"
~ Philip Larkin

I blame this instantaneous grief on the velvet-heavy
silk of dreams, unweaving the days, making space
for your severed body to grow back into sweetness
inside me.

Dreams ring your name from the long
unspoken journey, hunt for your syllables like an animal
on the trail of her own bloodied limb.

The witchcraft of love.

The belief that this is a real little girl,
lacerates my bones, *holds me*
like a heaven. Maybe I should blame the flickers
on the monitor. The fetal pole that won't grow
into heartbeats. I should blame you.

You rough-tongued siren, holding the nevers
of your life in one long, heavy, steady note.
Keeping me sailing toward that sound.

Or could it be that you are too salted
with the magic of your parents, with Texas and Haiti,
sunscrubbed from the womb, you spoke folded buds
and now your flowering absence buries me
in an unhurried precise suffering.

I must thicken.

Thicken into the great great granddaughter
of the slaves almanacked in my skin,
and understand that you are a tiny fish
destined to swim from me to the ocean.

You are my un-made daughter,
an amalgam of unfenced bougainvillea
and tornadoes, elements that sour
with a mirage of reds, unhushing the air—

A Cotton Field in Crosbyton Texas

silence tastes like red sand
                                          listen as it rattlesnakes
at the base of the cacti
the plants' posture off-green
beneath the butter-yellow Crosbyton sun

quiet threads through the canyon
back and forth over the wind
in and out your throat, crevices

no one screams here
because there is cotton   a plantation of clouds
spread stagnant over red earth
some of the buds brick red
with earth-mud as if the body
of the ground were hemorrhaging

I didn't hear an echo
no ghost hymns on the wind
not even after crouching
to pick a fiber from the bolls

Part III

Song for Making the Birds Come

In the late evening of a spring, she slips through
the thatch roof, the dust encrusted solidarities,

with fingers. Her rivulets adorn the fibers
of hay, parched crimson from sunlight—she comforts

them with a cool tenderness before the tip and pause,
the moment when she drops

round. Her song pounds the earth's brown
into a muddied sweetness.

Mojito Love, After Hurricane Katrina

tonight
i need mojito love
i need to come
with the bloom
of peppermint
(fresh cut)
in this hotel room
on Tennessee street

i want our tongues
to climax on rhum
our sweetened throats
hoarse
and drowning the mating
screech of rats
and cockroaches
on Canal street
nearby

please

coax this jazz
into your mouth
suck the mold
from the torn bricks
the one-legged barbie doll
the mud brown
Bagdad sign
please

suck them all up
into mint leaves

Move on moonlight, this is just another failed love poem

Banana and breadfruit are not enough.
In your mouth, they sour. Even the flesh
of the avocado, yellowing to brown.
How I would like to transition like that,
learn to unfasten my skin. You speak Cerulean
and serenade me, your voice waxing across
my hipbones. Already, I bellydance
to your lexicon. But it is not enough.

So tonight, I am practicing wishing you
sorrow. I need this moon to surrender the night.
Perhaps the plains of Lubbock, Texas
could simply quiet the moonlight. Let loose
the stench of cows and cattle feed.

Release the frat boys and their midnight pilgrimage
to orgies and God, all anointed in Heineken.
Nothing better than 18 year olds high on fucking
and Jesus to make you forget.

But the city relinquishes nothing
beyond the velvet of moonbeams
texturing the night. And I watch my cats,
watch them tear the reminiscences
of a stranger from a condom. Each tear of latex, each spill
of semen on to the carpet loosens the fists
behind my eyes. These are not tears.
Simply olive oil rushing out of me.

In the Backyard

Our breaths gift frozen angels to the night, to the Sahara-quiet of
the backyard, the dead celosia and the dying periwinkle

where language is lost.
Have things become too untellable?

The fabric of our voices used to be so sinuous
we spoke Haitian rhum, fairytales, and baseball.

"Noland Ryan threw no-hitters in his 40s," you said,
and I pretended to understand what that meant,

understood this game was your blur of poetry.
Your chest moved into mine, and our throats veined with lust,

with deep rusted secrets signing their way out our bodies,
eager to embrace Neruda, his having left scars on both of us

but we've become separate skins.
I quiver in slivers of lightening now, exist in tones.

Everything between my ribs, pushed and pressed into sediment.
My life quieting, ghosting into the barely living.

Your lips and your tongue are more green inchworms, you speak
And the hungry inchworms wriggle,

Torn between sex and not wanting children,
Sex and dishes, sex and anything.

A slaughterhouse of unkeepable sounds.

A Couple of Halves

Come over here she said with a bruised, quiet kindness,
shapeless like olive oil, needing to unlearn
what she already knew.

This is okay?
He asked.

They both knew it wasn't, but she allowed
her mouth to go against her body, to speak in tones
that translated her descent into sadness with erect nipples.

And he moved between the different feels of her,
the silk commotion of her skin, dark with moonlight
 and last month's miscarriage.

He knew what he would find inside her mouth,
whisper-breathings he wouldn't like the texture of, her saliva
half-manna, half poison with the lilt of children,

marriage, mortgage. The ripple and linger effect
of these words, the way they leaned into life,
into a language he never cared to learn,

but he needed to feel just right tonight, needed
his own lawless orgasm, so he allowed his body
to falter with hers, their skins determined

to embrace the elsewhere
they both carried within them.

Twilight. Layette, Louisiana

Live Oak branches crimson a sky
highlighted in flamingo strokes

Silken grey strands wrap around
bald cypress trees,

The Spanish moss still hoping to belly dance
to the last strand of indigo blue.

For Erzuli, Goddess of Love

My home is now where you are, so nectar on this hour
like the malachite butterfly. Arms braided beneath my breasts,
burrow your tongue, say I taste like rosemary and rosehips
while twilight gathers smoke-like over the canyons, the landscape
rough.
Your name and my name liquid on the russet night.

You are better at peacefulness and sleep than I. Devouring and
religious,
I smolder in our sheets like a jailed convict, twister-storms hissing
my way ready to anoint me in sweetgrass, pink hibiscus, and a
cayenne-pepper
halo of mosquitoes feeding off wet heat, the kind of burning
West Texas cannot understand, sieve-like skins

slick with the stench of burnt bark, the holy spirit, and ripe
sticky grenadine seeping through. The Goddess traces the calabash
roundness of my waist and buttocks, and I am driven half-mad
with words,
words that engrave love, ensoul the meaning deep in my sinews.

Our Road of Song

We are an embrace of tornadoes
and bougainvillea, you and I. We know dust
and moonlight gorged with heat.
You whisper autumn-red storms
into my ear and the voice of the desert
plains leaves me sandscrubbed, ablazed
with the sanguine Texas landscape.
Your fingertips wave over me, the shape
 of hailstones clustering over the half-moon
of breast, a wrinkled areola.
My tongue escapes its thicket to moisten
your tongue with silent races, with the reality
of the voracious Caribbean wind,
its canticle of ash and history.
We kiss until our mouths foam with what God
wants, shaking the crimson from the blood-
red bougainvillea. We kiss until we enter
poetry.

Une Nuit sur une Plage Haitienne

Shaded beneath the sky's suede under-garments,
sand-choked stars reflect the genteel moonlight,
chipped and cobalt-rimmed.

Moonstruck beams, ever silver in their silence,
melt across the ocean's breast, searing blue
goose bumps over the hiss of all round waves.

Stitched through an interstellar pattern, the silver flakes
wrinkle the night's latticework with threaded
cyan tears, almost staining the woolen air, diamond indigo.

After earning her MFA from Chatham College in Pittsburgh Pennsylvania, **Nimi Finnigan** decided to pursue a PhD in Literature with an emphasis in Creative Writing at Texas Tech University in Lubbock, Texas. Her essays explore her village, Camp-Perrin, in the south of Haiti where magic and myth are part of everyone's daily routine while place and identity are at the center of each of her poems—Haiti, Pittsburgh, or West Texas. Nimi's poems and essays have appeared in *The Meadowland Review, Journal of Caribbean Literature, The Lindenwood Review* and *Rosebud*, among others. She currently teaches at South Plains College in Lubbock, Texas while raising two daughters (and getting ready for a third one in March 2016) with her husband, Roderick.

www.ingramcontent.com/pod-product-compliance
Lightning Source LLC
Chambersburg PA
CBHW060224050426
42446CB00013B/3157